Civil
Insolencies

Civil
Insolencies
Bob Beagrie

**STACK
BOOKS**

Smokestack Books
1 Lake Terrace, Grewelthorpe, Ripon HG4 3BU
e-mail: info@smokestack-books.co.uk
www.smokestack-books.co.uk

ISBN 9781916012172

Smokestack Books
is represented
by Inpress Ltd

'From such rude principles our form began;
And earth was metamorphosed into man'
John Dryden

Contents

The Golden Age

'Needless was written law, where non opprest:
The law of Man was written on his breast.'
John Dryden, *Ovid's Metamorphosis, 1717*

a choice poised on the nib of a pen
or the turn of a dial in the Tardis

to find the Golden Age by traversing
star-paths of the past or the future

although the navigation console is on the blink –
(is in urgent need of a new head gasket)

and we might just twist off in infinite spirals as if
we're riding a waltzer, yelling, *Spin us Mister!*

'cos its better, they say, than simply standing still,
so get us out of here, steer us back, before that and that...

and that time when *they* arrived, and the Conqueror
came to claim the land, take us back to the wapentake

to the time of tolerance; to the salmon run
to the days before nostalgia turned us bitter

do you recall our Cornucopia?
take us all the way back to Arcadia

how fair it was, how strong and stable –
how we lived in isolation, secure in knowing

one's rightful place and what was expected
of firmly held borders between me, you, them.

or else spin us forward to *Gullaldr*, not otherwise
or elsewhere, when all the feuds are settled,

without neglect nor contempt and endeavours
are governed by the just cause of commonality

take me there and I'll not doff my hat
nor tug upon a forelock, if I have one.

The Historian's Reply

it would be
so great,
wouldn't it,
to be able
to travel back
to those
times?

No
    they   were
awful!   Truly
    truly
       terrible!

Real Remnants of Fictive Wars

after Cyprien Gaillard

'Tis not the laurel tree that brings
Anointing oil for sacred kings;
Those princes see the happiest days
Whose olive branches stand for bays.'
Aurelian Townsend, *Albion's Triumph, 1632*

No one spoke of the cloud,
though Maria played delightfully on the virginal
and sang, and somebody complemented her voice,
'Exquisite' was one word used, another was 'Unearthly'.
We ate. We drank.
When Sophia laughed she gave an involuntary little snort
that took her, and Charles, by surprise,
but no one spoke of the cloud.

It was a foggy, damp old day to begin with.
Mist hung heavily in the grounds
but the cloud on the lawn was whiter, starker
more alien, spreading quite disturbingly beneath
the conversation which acknowledged
the flock wallpaper, Lady Dampier's ball gown
Phillip's new pure bred and how all the children grow.

While the cloud unfurled like a pallid octopus in tissue paper
locked into a silent skirmish with itself, until
thankfully it appeared to strangle itself
and the trails and fronds drifted away
toward the damp trees and the ornamental lake,
and, fortunately, no one thought it necessary
nor reasonable to mention it.

Caveliero

There'd always been the stable's heavy smell
the animal warmth, neighs, whinnies and his
Da's soothing tones, that eased his *lovelies*,
settled their nerves while currying their coats,
picking their hooves, tacking them up for service;
and first he had watched and learned, then helped,
so became, over years, one with them, familiar,
he rode them, read them, dreamed, sometimes,
he was one, tailed and maned, as alert as liquid
to change; the quick skitter and flashes of wild
but Da' favoured the company of horses over folk,
thought more of them than his wife and his boy
(or that's how it always seemed), so like father
like son, when the Bishop's War began Robert
became a Dragoon under the Lord on the Hill.

Muster

'Then for ever rejoice,
When I've heard the voice
That the King enjoys his own again
Yes, this I can tell
That all will be well
When the King enjoys his own again'
Martin Parker, *When the King enjoys his own again, 1643*

The King's Man professed there'd be food aplenty,
companionship, glory, and he was bound to aid
his Majesty out of due obedience, and what, with
his family dead did he have to lose, better to serve
our gracious Sovereign's person and assist him in
bringing this revolt by ill-effected bodies to an end.
For all good men must oppose these trained bands
of militia who would to bring the Kingdome to ruin,
and there be opportunities for the faithful:
spoils, advancement, riches, properties.

Snowfall. Frostbite. Starvation.

James Mytton feeds another log onto the fire, for her
who dwells in dirt, and his boy dispersed in bark,
who he sang to in his sickness, bid him farewell
before the march to Newburn's mayhem to strike
the Covenanters; smoke him out; let her rise –
cauterise this raw wound – glimpse their faces
in the living red, in ash flakes, gurning to return.

Undertone

The knack is to master the blend, the hold,
the merge with latent stillness that reigns
before and after, the swift dissolve, slow
drift – the body become breath, and takes
the patience of a yew, in root-creep, hoof-
settle, light-dapple, I have snailed within
a stone's throw of regiments at rest, they
have stomped by me, unseeing, but a bill's
shaft away, disturbing crows that foretold
their coming amid wood pigeon clatter;
in this way I watch hate's tumours grow –
as shade absorbing change, like moss, that
flits away to feed it down the scuttlebutt:
I bear word of a gathering at Guisborough.

Miss Conception

On a tree stump across the firelight from Robert Cook
by Mytton's disgruntled slump, sits an abomination,
although neither are aware since she has proved adept
at concealing her Popery along with her wicked cunny
beneath the ruffled pleats of her scarlet pantaloons;
the quiet lad who stirs the pot, eschewing notions
of modesty, the slippery eel, this mockerie of man,
'Is that rabbit stew ready, Henry?' Mytton asks,
the monster-wench simply nods, Henry rarely speaks,
born of transgression, fed on the roots of vengeance;
yet if she were a true *monstre* would she not place her
unruly self on show as a freak of Bartlemew Faire?
No, she blends in well among these gentlemen of lace
collars, frilly cuffs, feathered hats and long loose hair.

The Brewing

ANNE: What time do ye' call this abolished hour?
Where's tho' been till now?

JACOB: I skipped o'er to hear the Grindle speak at
Upleatham.

ANNE: And what did she speak?

JACOB: Plenty, she claims the reckoning's on's way.

ANNE: I can see that, Mesen.

JACOB: But we be free without need for atonement
and should walk in't quietus.

ANNE: And should we join the likes o' the elect
we're likely to last through these turmoils?

JACOB: That's the crop.

ANNE: And tho' weren't seen?

JACOB: Nay lass, I was an undertone. But there's
ample men on the move. Something's brewing
tonight.

ANNE: Then we'd best squirrel the girls int' lader.

The Slippery Slide

'You're coming down fast
You're coming down fast
You're coming down fast
Yeah yeah yeah'
John Lennon/Paul McCartney, 'Helter Skelter', 1968

After an authoritative imposition
and the subsequent reactions

(knee-jerk spasms
and considered oppositions)

come initial blusters
of discontent, pricked pride

and the proclamations
of honour besmirched,

an assertion of a birth-right,
a blinkered belief in a common goal

re-stitching fabricated traditions,
bloodlines, the pointing out

of a perceived menace,
a festering grudge,

the hoisting of a banner
to marshal around,

a slogan, a strategy, a tactic,
a distinguishing sign of difference,
declarations of treachery –
a name for them, a name for us,

arguments grounded
upon undisputed hierarchies,

a source of finance, a system
for manipulating news, views,

distractions from the cracks
running through the ideal,

enforced repressions,
breaches in a code of conduct

public punishments, reprisals,
a dislocation of established boundaries,

destruction, loss, banishments,
a frantic exchange of roles

as perpetrator/victim,
random justifications, then

harvestings on barren fields, mutilations
multiplied, squared, cubed,

atrocities, burials, hauntings,
...attempted forgettings.

The Burnings

The monster recalls the Godly mob
ablaze with righteous indignation
at indulgences wilfully practiced
under licence of permissible leisure;

pointing the finger, stabbing the sky,
lighting torches, spitting shrapnel,
igniting The Book of Sports
in preparation for wayward bodies,

to reform the borders of acceptability,
rectify the correct codes of conduct,
to take back control, and thereby hand
it over to our duly elected legislators

deemed above all to know best
through disguised impartiality;
so, she kept her pretty head low,
held her breath in the priest hole

flinched as they tore down the May Pole,
up-turned the market stalls, bellowed
for blood, she spied devils in their frenzies
'though they claimed to do Christ's work.

Forced March

'This ae nighte, this ae nighte,
Every nighte and alle,
Fire and fleet and candle-lighte,
And Christe receive thy saule.'
The Lyke Wake Dirge (traditional)

From Malton across hail-lashed heatherlands:
Kirkbymoorside, Blakey Ridge, Castleton,
the cut of Ruthergate down through Kemplah Wood
to the remainder of the cross; devouring mile-markers,
bridestones, megaliths, The Lord's wind in his face,
Hugh Cholmley drives his pack of war dogs onward
with the whip of his words, *On, Rogues and Rufflers,*
it is the First Fruits of the Spirit that shall nourish us!
with Whitby, his home, under threat these hounds
with round heads and sheathed steel teeth
(cony-catchers, apple-squires, nips, cross-biters)
refuse to rest, each stride bringing them closer
to salvation, their own and that of a divided nation
through hallucinations of exhaustion, fear, trembling.

The long ditch calls in a voice of earth,
Roll in, curl up, lai doon yoe hedds
spek what yoer nehst sore step is worth
the's little to gaaign at this road's end
drop yoer burdens, stay 'ere insteed
anly death awayts aheed me freonds.

Procession

'...for I see the dirt of the Slough of Despond
is upon thee; but that slough is the beginning
of the sorrows that attend those that go on in that way.'
John Bunyan, *Pilgrim's Progress*, 1678

Tinker John is tramping in the train of boots
through porridge spills of freezing fog
a lousy sun crawling from its make-shift cot
sick-bed, scruff-basket nest up on Ravenscar;
is only aware of something groaning deep
inside himself – it tells him he is still alive.
They clomp across the underside of clouds
their pikes and helmets scrape furrows
in the fields beside The Lion's beer garden –
you can glimpse them passing in the bull's-
eye bevel of the remote pub's snug window.
John remembers that one day he will beget
a daughter, blind-born meadow flower,
who shall inherit the Earth, like him,
through suffering, in this topsy-turvy world
he's learning how to live on the invisible.

This Commotion

By the Roda Cross Sir Hugh calls a brief halt
to let the troop catch its breath, foot and horse
find respite, while gunners check the cannon
remains secure and stable on the back of a wagon,
swig a sip from a hipflask to stoke the belly's fire,
nibble at yellow gorse flower, eye barren skylines:
a tattered cloud – sun beams flood Cockayne Ridge
to signal a land of plenty, a common treasury
kept out of reach by the trappings of majesty.
Then, a drab heath-hen bursts frantick to low flight
wings awhir, beak klop-klop-kloping proclamations
over sheep droppings, *It is the will of the people!*
Are we not all, John thinks, grouse bred for the rifle,
heirlooms of the Land Lords' pressed austerities?

Enemies of the People

'We had fed the heart on fantasies,
The heart's grown brutal from the fare,
More substance in our enmities
Than in our love...'
WB Yeats, *The Stare's Nest by my Window,*
from *Meditations in Time of Civil War*, 1922.

three grand owls
and whatever decision they'll make
the next chapter, though
it's yet to be drafted-written-revised

factious conventicles
those immersed a second time
remember Münster
          the horror   the terror
the troubles   the cache of weapons
buried in the woods for the just-in-case
expertise – its forecasts and explanations

the lie on the campaign bus
          so much
              misdirection, away
from an acceptance of history as gaps
the dead albatross you wear on your back

the girl with the Mata Hari stare
          tied to the stake refusing
a blindfold   all those
like them   remoaners
          big bad losers
Covernanters
          in the Killing Time
     traitors   malignants
          unpeople within the people
Cnut's wet socks and the incoming tide

Revelation

'...earth plastred with English goare and turned into a Golgotha of bones...'
Eye-witness account of Edgehill after the battle

Conscience squats the nape of each conscript
whispering babbles of doubt into their lugs, yet
since Edgehill Lieutenant Colonel Launcelot
has felt no trace of temerity for he knows
He hath stood upon Hellsmouth's bloody lip
peering into the pytt and perceived a trewth,
that turned his mortal meat to shafts of light
his ribcage to pearly gateposts through which
The Saved shall come to gladly pour their souls,
for he hast strode through carnage unscathed
with a dreadful calmness of the spirit
while all around him screamed and fell,
and he was saturated by God's Grace,
who revealed how he be the Christ reborn –
how this world of muck, steel, blood, smoke
be naught but the flit of tallow-cast shadow;
these grunts have yet to undergo such baptism.

Scarecrows

'If anyone on the verge of action should judge himself according to the outcome, he would never begin.'
Søren Kierkegaard, *Fear and Trembling,* 1843

Will Coppe, sitting on a lichen slab, spits
on the earth, grounds the spittle into the dirt
with one boot sole, takes a bite of a biscuit
hands John what's left, neither of them speak.
Since conscription they have both destroyed
many straw men with blade and musket balls
in the training grounds of Scarborough Castle
but with Edgehill's mowing an oft whispered
Hellmouth of sinners shovelled into Doom's Mill,
the prospect of destroying folk made up of skin
and bone sticks in the craw like biscuit crumbs.
Yet convincement is signed in each fellow's
Book of Conscience for The Lamb's War you
must know before you witness his Kingdome.

The Passenger

'rebellion is as the sin of witchcraft'
Samuel 25.23

*'we have also multitudes of witches among us... More, I may well say,
than ever this Island bred since the Creation, I speak it with horror.'*
Epistolae Ho-Elianiae: The Familiar Letters of James Howell, *1646*

Hunched like a sack of black powder,
on the horse drawn wagon that holds
the roped-down minion, sits the witch
or that's what Will Coppe claims she be
They'll not leave this up to the might
of men, arms and God, but of witchery!
although the tinker boy has his doubts.
So, as their boots eat the heathland miles
John keeps an eye on the shrouded one,
spots strands of smoke beneath the veil
one wizened claw, his hackles bristle
when he senses her glare swing his way,
discounts a snatch of some incantation
like plague-soot adrift on hoar draughts.

Chiromancy

'The great Sage as high as Heaven visited here.'
Wu Cheng'en, *Journey to the West,* 1592

High staggered moorland crossroads
too few trees, the big wide sky
fresh roadkill and opportunist crows
turning turning turning turning,
The Roda Cross by the roadside
scattered offerings in the grass
Hogtenberg's summit beyond Westerdale
Crouched friars, Rosedale Abbey, Cockayne Ridge
Roundhead recruits resting sore shanks,
tarmac's scrape and sweep through crimples:
Life line, Fate line, Heart line, Sun line.

The cross's shadow pointing arrow straight
at Boulby Mine, turbines and the sea
turning turning turning turning,
sheep picking paths through cropped heather,
fleeces marked with red or blue splodges,
lichen forests spreading over dry stone walls.
I stand, one hand on the cross, turning,
aiming names at horizon markers
knowing the words can't reach them,
how the crow-wind strips them bare,
how history is deciphering our footprints.

The Great Commission

'...the Eternall and shortly-expected King shalt open the clouds to judge the severall Kingdomes of the world...put an end to all Earthly Tyannies.'
John Milton, *Of Reformation*, 1641

Moor-light sharpened to a cut throat razor,
hair-fronds of mist coiling up the cliffs
from scrubs of stubble over nab and boulder
towed by a wafting that stings each iris,
teases out a clear, single-minded trickle;
Will Coppe announces to any who'll hear,
'*We be dwelling, brothers, at the End of Days,
are we not, all of us, God's soldiers tasked
to bed the ground for Christ's Second Coming,
to make ready for hys Final Dyspensation –
we be heralds of the Rapture! Wilt thee
Tinker John be number'd amongst the elect
or wander lost through lands the Blessed
have left*?' But John is busy contemplating
the University of the Firmament in a frozen
puddle, cracks it with his heel as he stands
to Cholmley's call to march on to Kildale.

Hidden Treasures

A cellar in a farmhouse in Hutton Locras,
its doorway concealed by an oak cupboard,
Aunt Anne perched by the scullery shutter
peering for the advancement of anyone.
Underneath her feet, beneath the proggy mat
Elizabeth and Margery skulk without candle,
quiet as spiders, their softness safe as snails
in shells till the troops vacate Craven Vale.
'We shalt not risk any Rebel nor Caveliero to
commit insolencies upon ye, both sides be men –
they have tongues like angels but cloven feet.
Stir not, but pray to God with breath alone.'
Stirrups straining, five days, four nights abode,
while iron shod hooves hammer the dirt road.

Werewolves

Little Robert Cook, a Pennyman's man, warms
bare feet by the campfire while cleaning his gun,
overhears the echo of his Mam's soft scolding,
'Ye'll gee yersel' chilblains like that my Son!'
ramming the rod topped with tow into the muzzle
that spat a ball, last year, into a Scotsman's face,
he watches the stars and wonders how they appear
in Newe Engeland where he wishes, one day, to go
once Parliament's discourtesy to The King's person
is quelled, its chief instigators all tried and hanged,
but first he'll lend a hand to the restoration of peace
in the name of the rightful father of the nation.
Barrel, breech oiled he checks the stock and butt
he hammered 'gainst that cottage door last night,
him and James Mytton, just having a bit of fun
with the locals, insisting on spoils like courteous
wolves, slunk back to camp with a full saddlebag
of silver, the old cottager left with a broken nose.

Spoils

'We are all the most abominable plunderers, I am ashamed to look an honest man in the face.'
Colonel Arthur Goodwin, 1642

ROBERT: Bit much that was, mate.

JAMES: Nah man, he was asking for it.

ROBERT: It's one thing taking their gear, that's only fair...

JAMES: I was promised spoils, all's I've got's a dose of piles.

ROBERT: ...that's what I'm saying, but smacking 'em about is a step too far.

JAMES: I didn't like the way he was looking at me, and besides, a smack in the nose is the least of his troubles. Folks 'll see a stack more than that in the coming months, I tell you.

ROBERT: Well, it settled 'em both for sure.

JAMES: This is our pilgrimage Rob. This is gonna set me on high and take you over the big water.

ROBERT: I get the feeling they're still hiding sommat, though.

JAMES: We could nip back and put a bit more pressure on 'em. He'll likely crack if we give his old bag a slap or stick a pistol barrel down his throat.

ROBERT: Did ye hear what she said?

JAMES: Who?

ROBERT: The Old Dear. She said sommat as we left, muttered under her breath.

JAMES: Didn't catch it.

ROBERT: Sounded like a hex.

JAMES: You saying she's a witch? Pick up a stone, die in a ditch.

ROBERT: It's like her eyes wanted to eat my whole life.

JAMES: Well I heard nowt, but like I said, we can pay 'em another visit, see what it is they're hiding.

ROBERT: Nah, she gives me the skitters, let's leave it for tonight. We can split this back in the tent and call it a day.

Milk Flowers

Huddled on the bank
hidden within the treeline
Captain Medley squats,

rests his back against
an elm's sinuous trunk –
sturdy as his father's thigh

when he hugged it before
it left for Bohemia
and the White Mountain –

there is movement
down there
behind the swine feathers

time now to wait, take stock
in readiness
and ease their aching feet.

They will not speak
other than
with hands and numb fingers;

beside his knee he spots
a fragile cluster, sagging heads:

Dew-Drops, Naked Maidens,
Snow-Piercers, Gillow-Herbs
Death Bells, White Queens;

objects of dread
or tokens of hope?

Deformation

'What a monstrous birth flows from thy fruitfull wombe...'
John Hockluyt, *An Alarm for London*, 1647

The monster's mother had many Popish pictures,
icons and crucifixes in which she much delighted
spent many hours in prayer to gain God's blessing
and in other corruptions and superstitions of faith,
partook readily of the sacrament and in the foolery
of fetes, which maketh her loathsome in the eyes
of the Babe of Grace, and who much admired Queen
Henrietta and harboured in her heart a hope she could
bring both King and Country back to the fold of Rome,
she oft gave liberty to carnal and sensual pleasures,
her mouth was known to utter intolerable heresies –
insisted upon calling The Lord's Day Sunday, until
the Puritans landed in the parish tasked to demolish
all traces of idolatry, cleanse the churches of such
affections, breaking stained glass, burning effigies
of the Virgin; who treat her coarsely though far from
uncivilly in order to open her eyes, and in their zeal,
stripped bare as a new born babe, whipped her raw,
had their way, then sliced the ears off her familiar,
the shock of which the monster's mother did never
recover, so Corporal Alice was hatched from atrocity
although she went under the counterfeit of Henry.

Keeping a Safe Distance

'...Nor yet stayed the terror there,
Infernal ghosts, and hellish furies, round
Environed thee, some howled, some yelled, some shrieked'
John Milton, *Paradise Regained,* 1671

May calves skitter and gambol across the field
where the public footpath leads from the gate
up to the skirt hem of the forest, and the mature
cows stare at us from wells of bulbous blackness
weighing us up, they sway off in a milk-heavy plod
tugging the intangible leads of their young, we wait
not wanting to rile them, then one stops, swinging
her skull back over her shoulder, lets out a long
mournful bellow, once, twice, three times before
her gangly offspring trots out from behind the trees
to trail her to the safer side of the meadow away
from Sunday afternoon strollers, lycra-clad cyclists,
and those invisible ones who are still creeping low
from the dank fringe to take aim and wait the order.

His Mere Creature

'Though the earth, and all inferior creatures,
be common to all men, yet every man has a property
in his own person: this no body has any right to but himself.'
John Locke, *The Second Treatise on Civil Government*, 1660

Tinker John surveys the world of rime
down the matchlock's barrel, disregarding
the herd of dairy dowagers and their calves,
the May wanderers, skeletal contraptions
the Range Rover with the UKIP sticker
on the rear bumper parked up on the verge –
phantasms of the periphery; instead rests
his whole attention on the collection of Gentlemen
bivouacked down in the dell, knows well Heaven
and Hell lie cheek to cheek between his ears –
twin sides of a sovereign held under his tongue.
Powder in the priming pan, cover closed, slow-
match lit, ready to dip into the serpent's jaws.
Salus Populi Suprema Lex.
In this dawn-light we'll right the sins of devils –
his first taste of an unappealing sacrifice,
hammer poised, his finger strokes the trigger.

Aunt Anne's Canticle for Calm

'Lay by your pleading, law lies a-bleeding
Burn all your studies down, and throw away your reading
Small power the word has, and can afford us
Not half so much privilege as the sword does'
The Dominion of the Sword, Cavalier Ballad from *Rump Songs,* 1686

Close your eyes, my dears, to the wailing
turn the locks, my loves, to your hearing
to rumbles that run through the ground
an anthem of gunshot and mortuary swords
hoof beats, orders, the barking of hounds
the lengthening quiet between roars,
the stricken chewing churned grass in the field
our doorway is sealed with a scouring
of thistles and stinging nettles. Lie still
within the darkness, covered by a sheet
pay no heed as night limps from Ruthergate
to settle on a log to catch its breath,
stretch its legs and count the day's cost
in a volley of owl hoots across the clearing,
turn the locks, my dears, to your hearing.

Justification of the Mad Crew

'*The abondon'd race, transformed to beasts, began*
To mimick the impertinence of Man.'
Samuel Garth, *Aeneas Descends to Hell*, 1717

'*...by the mere fact that he forms part of an organised group, a man*
descends several rungs in the ladder of civilisation. Isolated, he
may be a cultivated individual; in a crowd, he is a barbarian...
acting by instinct. He posesses the spontineity, the violence, the
ferocity, and also the enthusiasm and heroism of primitive beings.'
Gustav Le Bon, *Psychologie des foules*, 1895

At the signal snowflakes fall into the camp
of fellow creatures to become one flesh.
Brass drakes are monkeys who shall neither
see evil, know evil or act evil, but howl
growl and spit fiery flying shot, conduct
their rightful function, like fusiliers, pikemen –
there being no such thing as sin in any
outward acts so long as love's light is held
within and the knowledge that all things
are pure to the pure, like how a battle
sings of metamorphosis, marking all
who enter, a chorus of brainsick men
prance in absurdum – a motion of the spirit,
to find where a soul resides within them.

At times like this, what matters?

'Then to see legs and arms torn ragged fly
And bodies gasping, all dismembered lie.'
George Lauder, *The Scottish Soldier*, 1629

all the knots in the weave that brought each
combatant here, what knocks and cares
that shaped who they thought they were,
and wherever their threads might lead,
evaporates like night sweat on oak leaves
in the Rift Woods when the Sun breaks
over the cliff, moon swimming in a bowl
of broth, equine dreaming, a new mother's
clothes burned in the fire, a baby crying
into the night as if it knew, fresh rumours
of the plague, sparks of brimstone from
the pulpit, the pull of the pilgrim: when life
is squeezed to a flash on the killing field:
a step, a glance, a thrust, a dash of luck?

Ord'nance

'Behold, I give unto you the authority to tread on serpents and scorpions, and overcome all the power of the enemy: and nothing shall by any means hurt you.'
Luke 10: 19

i)

The valley shatters as an empty
crystal glass rains
its contents upon the table top

shards of inheritance
make a constellation of cinders
Capricorn powered by Mars

the heart's chambers
packed with black powder
ignited in a spasm

to live like a thunder clap
given a familiar name
and score its mark on memory

ii)

windage
the gap between projectile and bore
propellant gas
a hare's breath between friend and foe

through recoil and momentum
each body rolls
backward – forward
caught in vibrations of transference

but where does it go,
this drive for obliteration
once the fight is over?

There are new holes for hiding
wide open mouths
fresh wounds to fester in.

The Mummers Play

'His fires beheld, and sickening,
Hid their strong limbs in smoke.
For with noises ruinous loud;
With hurtlings & clashings & groans
The Immortal endur'd his chains,
Tho' bound in a deadly sleep.'
William Blake, *The Book of Urizen,* 1794

Clothed in fire, Guilford Slingsby hovers mid-fall
punched by a cannon's blast right out of his form
turning in air, a murmuration of dislodged particles
catching the wind and dispersing, whatever's left
begins to shower the frozen ground: flesh-spots
and bone-stones in parcel-wraps of skin and cloth;
but how can he mind, enraptured as he is by dancers
all about him? Watch them wading through tides
of space-time, bereft of any rhyme or reason behind
the wrenboys guise; fixated on those other soulers
reeling in the currents of a lovers' tempest, up there
above his shell-stunned skull. Did he hear them
call to him? Not the name for the ruined husk-thing
that collapses into mud, but one he'd long forgotten.

Visitation

'...and behold, there came up among them another little horn...in this horn were the eyes of man, and a mouth speaking great things... and shall wear out the saints... and think to change times and laws and they shall be given into his hand until a time and times and the dividing time.'
Daniel, 7.8, 21–25

After two days Elizabeth begins to quiver
to moan, mutter and when Margery tries
to quiet her with strokes and soothing sounds,
covers her with a quilt she throws it off
with her shift and writhes naked in darkness,
'I am ful of paynes, ful of thundr and lihtining!'
She gasps, *'He is here, can thee not see him sistr? –*
a wyrm of grete dyspeyr, one wyth the small horn
to piyrce us both wyth schame, ofering in hys
insolens hys tetys for us to swukyn, the gostlie
enmy has comyn, hath layth hys snar of letchery
and woud mayke me hys wyfe, oh, ayd me sistr
for hys flecshy lust wyll not be qwenchyd,
I am afeared he has com to tayk my sowle!'

Shroud

'Give them not praise. For, deaf, how should they know
It is not curses heaped on each gashed head?
Nor tears. Their blind eyes see not your tears flow.
Nor honour. It is easy to be dead.'
Charles Hamilton Sorley, *When You See Millions of the Mouthless*
Dead, 1916

On the day they made war
snow was a Godsend
the way it softly-softly covered up
the results without discrimination –

in case anyone was tempted to look back
at the morning or any of the days before.

All afternoon shudders could be brushed off
as being on account of the cold
and the only talking point was about:

how long it would fall
how thick it would lay
how deep you would sink
if you ventured out onto
the field of tumbling crows.

Each day after
they worried what the melt might show –
things with no name shorn of time, weather
stars, trinkets and other such spoils.

Clay Pipe

Turned up
in the old pungence of soil
in the farthest worm-wave
of the new ploughed field

Delicate
as bird-bone fragments
stained pieces of pleasure:
bore, bit and a barley twist

Moon-shards
shed scales of stiffened cloud,
congealed smoke rings;
the curds and whey of waiting

Stern lip
unsmiling and toothless
dropped in sudden fluster
at the first drum's stammer

Stem cracked
underfoot as the cold dawn
breaks and the sun's glow
bleeds out over the river mouth.

Lyke Wake

'Where am I hurried! What sanguine place
Is this I breathe in, garnished with disgrace?'
John Quarles, *An Elegy upon that Never to be Forgotten Charles*
the First, 1649

The broken men yield, after the blizzard's rage,
to the scandal of disorder, tainted by the taste
of this new age and grub about for tales to give
account for their phantasmagoria from ordinary
house-holder, groom, apprentice, tinker, gent,
undisciplined idler rendered citizen-soldier,
hystericals, histrionics, mama's boys, bastards,
brewers, patricides – although there is so much
they'll not meddle with, including themselves,
having been shunted out of grammar's backdoor
into the vulgar dirt of unpronouncables, the fylth-
riddled freedom of formlessness, succoured on
an homeopathy of killing. Their dark nativities
bubble with ramblings to take back control
in defence of the state as Cartemandua, Frigg
Britannia, safe-guarded, wearing the familiar
mask of mother, sweetheart, favourite whore –
each of them a springhead of fresh anxieties,
labour pains for a post-term Kingdom Come.

Mercurial Rusticus

'Then said the Interpreter, You must learn of this sheep to suffer,
and to put up wrongs without murmurings and complaints.'
John Bunyan, *Pilgrim's Progress,* 1678

After such Barbarous Outrage upon
this once flourishing crinkle of the realm
he is borne upon a litter over
the roaring straights of malaise to be
laid on a table in some rustic barn,
whereupon Sir Hugh Cholmley commands
the *Chyrurgeon* to implement his arts
to do what he might to tend his mangled
cousin, so between one strong man behind,
another before, the bloody foe is held
down to receive the great and terrible
instrument, sharpened, well-oiled, concealed
from view until the last instance, although
Guilford is swaddled in a fleece of feints.

Fugitive

Havoc stung, ears still ringing from the din,
Henry has squeezed inside the hollow trunk
of a burnt out tree to avoid the round up
and take stock, she has lost her dog lock pistol
and powder horn but has her rapier, a dagger
in her boot and a head swimming with wreckage,
torn men, spilt blood. Did she kill amidst the fray?
It's hard to tell within the swirl of battle-time
that's left her limbs like straw, her squirrel heart
caught in a snare, as loud as a war-drum
within the wooden womb. When night falls
she'll slip out restored, take the moors road
to Whitby with a will to secure the harbour
for Queen Henrietta Maria, alone if needs be.

Death Pools Each Breath

Guisborough Pastoral: 1643

January: not a choice month to be conducting
war – but needs must when *cruel necessity* calls;
musket smoke, churned mud, blood splashed snow fields,
icicles glisten on worn masonry,
gargoyles peer from de Brus's priory
at souls freshly plucked from suspect bodies
to loiter in the hedgerows, snagged on thorns
like tufts of sheep wool, musket smoke, hoar frost.
Roseberry is a drab, pitted finger
raised against the sky's God-given birth-right,
its fine white lace, its sumptuous wardrobe;
while Slingsby feints as the Physic saws
through femur, cauterises the raw stump,
starts on its twin. Each dark pooling breath.

Cruel Necessities

Robert Cook has collapsed in the garden plot
and cannot rise, turns the turnip patch red.
The girls in the cellar can hear his cries
Anne suspects, along with any good folk
in earshot, and the sod has left a spoor
along the track, the path and smeared her gate
to lead the pack straight to her nettled door step
(the charm's been known to work in peace time),
she'll not tolerate another rude visit now
the mowing has ceased, the round-up begun.
In desperation Anne, who already has more
than one skeleton in the back of her closet,
takes Jacob's spade in her flour white hands,
ventures from the scullery, stands above
the earthworm squirming in the mud,
his fingers trying to dam the spill of his guts.
The smell is not good. He is tossed upon
the high waves of the Atlantic, afeared
of drowning, Massachusetts still waiting.
Anne raises the spade to quieten the blighter
to put him out of his miseries, she'll hide
him in the woodshed and swill away his stains.

The Trembling Cup

'Nothing except a battle lost can be half so melancholy as a battle won.'
Horatio Nelson, 1805

Three days of slipping in and out of torpor,
due to the excess of humors, black and yellow
swaddled by the shakes and sweats of fever
ligatures strapped around the stumps, dressed
with egg yolk, oil of roses, turpentine.
Slingsby's mother is on her way to see her babe
while his breath still pools and Sir Hugh slumps
by the hearth in Prior Pursglove sipping blood
of the vine from a cup of tremors, eyes locked
on the conflagration that repeats-repeats-repeats
the butchery of his God-fearing country folk,
sees this calamity spreading through the shires
and the hundred and twenty prisoners penned
after their call for quarter, awaiting their fate.

Night of Temporary Stillness

'Thou shouldst go, leof, hop o'er te see Awd Nan
Jeannie o' Mulgrave till the wrath's blown out.'
Jacob sighs, his voice a chimney sprite as the pair
huddle beside their hearth's few flutterings –
just to crack the chill in the room, not enough
to draw attention, but Anne'll have none of it,
'I be flitting no place wi' the bairns down there,
asides, Man, thou stands more risk than I.
Thou should slip o'er te Tockets for a time.'
She pats his hand but knows he'll not budge,
he twitches his tender neb, winces, hooks
a cold finger around one of her's. She spots
a flame-hare dart across a charcoal field
of wheat; feels it's tug tickle, that old familiar
tingle but she'll not bolt; so hacks, gobs into
the hearth and they watch her spittle moon
drip and fizzle on the blackening kindling stack.

Anaesthesia

'Who warned you to flee from the coming wrath?'
Matthew 3:7

Sir Hugh lets his rabble of ironsides blow off steam
numb the brain and raw nerves with cheap liquor
give thanks they're not numbered among the dead –
time to scrutinise victory, survival and sacrifice.
Tinker John wracks his fuddled head for an antiphon
to things he witnessed within the thick of the push –
a thing that knelt in gore, fish scales, dragon wings
bear paws, a lion's maw, its umbilicus squirting fire
dowsing him with the grace to damn or bless.

It comes again as he struggles with sleep:

'As stones shalt cry, thou hast drunk
and eaten of war's meat and by its taste
shall upturn this time and times and half
a time from the roots of grass, and know
that all poor are one, and he is flailing
amid the miraculous dust and cannot
find the door, although should he exit,
poured out like water, he, as multitudes,
shalt find himself unbound and be a judge
to all – I have seen this before, thou too,
having seen all at a time when seeing
at once; having spoke all at a time when
speaking at once, gaze upon me, rejoice;
sing out with thine voyce and unvoyce.'

Next morning Cholmley leads a prayer to The Lord
before ordering the prisoners released to disperse
in peace, to go home or join their righteous cause,
'So together we may turn our sovereign's heart!'
Most drift off up onto Eston Hills, a few remain
realising as Upright Men – the sons of landless waifs
what's at stake, what must be done to displace a king.

Happy Hour

What holds us in the bar of the Black Swan
now the rain has stopped, the High Street
bathed in late afternoon sun, the stalls
packing up, the day's trading done, brown
in the glass with a good foamy head –
its substance attracts the matter of my lips,
the quiz show on the wall-mounted telly –
a hum, an Arts Nouveaux print for Absinth
by the window, the clock's slow hand stuck
on a roman numeral, makes me ponder
what held those men in place nearly four
centuries ago without a theory of gravity
(Isaac being not a fortnight old) – fear,
fealty or fresh sense of liberty. What held
them then – what holds us now? And soon
the boys'll pile in on the piss buoyed up
by bravado and centrifugal force with Big
Ginge already kicking off with Ryan
over a long simmering grudge about Britt,
spitting into his face, how, back in the day,
she may well have been a lap dancer,
but he's on the verge of losing it big time,
in fact he'll kill the smarmy cunt if ever
he clocks him ogling her like that again.

The Reaping

'Each regiment in order grows
That of Tulip, Pink and Rose...
But war all this doth overgrow
We Ord'nance Plant and Powder sow.'
Andrew Marvell, *Upon Appleton House*, 1651

'Degradation digs a bodily grave for a new birth; it has not only a
destructive, negative aspect, but also a regenerative one...'
Mikhail Bakhtin, *Rabelais & His World*, 1965

'The aim is, here in Britain, to create a really hostile environment...'
Theresa May, 2012

Remember when you dwelt within the Garden of Ecstatic Ferocities
where horticulture warped your frame into frills and petal folds?

Where your arms were burdened with clusters of ripe berries drooping
in a pulping sweetness that dripped through your tendril fingers?

Where you passed through splitting fruits and tangles of old growth,
lost yourself in explosions of colour from accelerating seasons?

How you left a litter-trail of new cuttings scattered upon the sward,
pollinated vacant, sticky stigma in casual acts of propagation?

How you romped in joyous abandon, spilling over deadwood,
trampled mulch, spliced and grafted unruly foreign bodies?

Do you recall the frenetic fight for light in the Garden of Exquisite
Furies where you learned the savage nature of predation?

How you conducted the rites of naming, suppressed weakness,
buried impoverishment, harvested fungal blooms in an iron helm?

How, daubed in charcoal and loam, you repelled invasive pests,
how poor Priapus's severed stalk re-seeded fallowed soil?

Where you were whetted by his semen, how you dug a trough
in earth-flesh and laid down within it to receive resurrection?

How could anyone fully suppress these exquisite ecstasies
or forget the furies and ferocities of this ever returning Eden?

The Things the Owls Observed

'A field after battle utters its own sound
Which is like nothing on earth, but is earth.'
Geoffrey Hill, *Funeral Music*, 1968

Temperamental eddies
of wind in the trees, an apprehensive
short-lived snowfall
    scurries
of a field mouse
in a hawthorn tangle
the sluck
of a black slug on October's
fallen trunk,
an abundance
of fresh meat –
its uncommon stink

horses quivering
in their own steam, the stamp
of a boot by a crackling brazier

discordant songs
of victory and camaraderie

Aunt Anne's kitlyn snuffling
pawing mewling
about the wood pile
the pond
locked by a guild of ice –
something moving
underneath

a fevered voice
muffled by a cellar's sunken
stone walls, the whimpers
of a thing
on the threshold of Hell

the Evening jig of a lone
pipistrelle

James Mytton
soil-smeared like Lazarus
rising
from a thicket, kneeling
in a shock of moon-slurry

his whispered prayer
I am delivered,
he stands, elected...

the scrunch
stump –
    scrunch –
stump –
of footsteps as he limps
the waters standing
on his cheeks
toward the illuminations
of the 24/7 filling station.

Cairn

'Our wrongs have armed us with such strength,
So sad is our condition
That could we hope that now at length
We might find intermission,
And had but we had before,
Ere these mechanics sway'd;
To our revenge, knee-deep in gore,
We would not fear to wade.'
Samuel Butler, *A Coffin For King Charles, A Crown for Cromwell*
and a Pit for the People, 1649

'What can they know that we know that know the time to die?'
WB Yeats, *The Curse of Cromwell,* 1936

i)

There is a sundered man
in a snow drift gully
up on Low Moor
above Birk Brow,
where the A171 slithers
between Lockwood
and Stranghow, crouched
in a state he cannot stomach
for he has partaken
in acts he struggles to grasp
for a thirst he could not slake,
over a cause he failed
to wholly gauge but for slogans,
promises, Lorelei's melody
that fired his fealty toward
a pedigree of *pater-familias* –
The Lord's direct line.

Does it matter now
why he felt obliged
to become an instrument
of slaughter, other than
how we might find ourselves
kneeling by his side
pondering why
such savagery overcame us?
Oh, I've felt the same urge
to wallow in bile though
found the wherewithal
to rein in its sting.

ii)

On the honeyed seam
of a frigid dawn,
they bind their tails
in makeshift uniform,
to raise a copse of pikes
about a standard,
sing anthems timed
to each left stride
as on they march
into the knackers yard,
Who are ye?
Who are ye?
Who are ye?

While Kingsmen skit-
scrabble amidst calls
for articles, effects,
misplaced demeanour:
doublet, cuirass, gloves,
helmet, boots and balls
some without socks,
some without pants,
the drummer boy cracking
the call-to-arms
as arquebus pellets
harass camp wives, whores,
dogs, cooking pots, fizz
like wound-up wasps;
and the first offering
to the turf agape
at latticed chemtrails
mouth drawn wide
enough to swallow
whole the sun's halo.

The Rightful Share

Will Coppe bids farewell to Tinker John
slaps his back and says '*God be with thee*,'
as, bolstered by the quarrelsome fires
of victory, the flickering embers of belly fear,
and with such little notion of the strings
of consequence that have been plucked
half of Cholmley's troop make preparations
to leave and trudge through slanting hail
toward Nunthorpe, Marton, Stainton, Yarum
to disrupt the Cavalier supply train
the Duke of Newcastle maintains with York
over the bridge to Egglescliffe, and there
to paint the river red, give an offering to Peg:
the seed of Cain battling agin their own kin.
They'll not set eyes on one another again.

Carrion Song for Major Tom

They took me in under the storm cloud's wing
fed me on fire, bid me level these barren heaths
with spade, rake, hoe
with spade, rake and hoe
in joined desire, we remove rough stones,
our fathers' scattered groans
layers of self we've sloughed off in growth,
dismembering ourselves, to stand alone
as Osiris or John Barleycorn
We turn, together, the soil of memory
compact years, smell ripe turf
Whatever shall we find as we finger the dirt?
spend hours sowing suns in common ground
to grow the pillars of Eden before sin,
as before my fall,
in rhymes of dipping scythes
sacks of sweat-won grain
and scarecrow grins wide as a rolling moor
Remember when, remember
when remembering
this remains an old battle scene,
a place for levelling men on points of swords,
over the fence we'll forever tear down

undermine, come each month's curdled cream,
through distances drawn up in murky pails
to our long-lost hanging grounds:
Doggerland,
Avalon, Lyoness,
Albion
poaching trails and corpse ways
still lead stray quails toward a mythic
sleeper dreaming under the golden hill –
not our King, divine, with his head lopped off,

his blue-blood-spill soaked in strips of cloth
and sucked on to ease a blight or bitter ache
to bring prosperity
to reverse a curse
but some starveling sovereign, low itinerant,
peasant-born pilgrim with a leaking song,
ear clipped, pilloried, with branded cheek,
or a departed starman crowned on Mars
with nothing left to lose
So, halt one moment in manuring, hear
those mouldwarps scurry to their Lazarus Palace,
secreting treasures beneath the grasses
shadow-cast by our booted soles
by our spades, rakes and hoes.

The Weigh-in

'Their wisdom's profound, to cheat us of our ground.'
Gerrard Winstanley, *You Noble Diggers All*, 1649

Take your share of tree moss and rock fur
The whistle of grass and dry poppy seeds
Nettle stings and tiny dust tornadoes
Take your share and store it safe

Take your share of new hues from bulbs
Splitting casings of sap-sticky buds
The golden petals of wee-the-beds
Take your share and garner it well

Take your share of a curl of river mist
A flat stone's skim and its final splash
A pupa dangling from its silken path
Take your share and keep it ripe

Take your share of the crumble and flake
A drip and its echo off in the dark
A shadow to wear as a shawl at night
Take your share and wrap it up tight.

The Yarm Troll

The old stone bridge steps over in four strides
splashing sandstone across the placid flow
but despite the name it is not the same river
the drawbridge and its sentries are long gone,
kids play ball on the well-trimmed lawn behind
the wind-touselled tresses of a weeping willow,
and it is hard, this sunny Sunday afternoon,
to comprehend the fury that turned neighbours
into foes, stamped the mark of Cain on some
and Abel's upon others, how bitterness breaks
its banks, sweeps up men like leaves in its flood,
how commoners are peddled the lie to stake
their lives on a future they all might treasure.
Beneath one arch, today, floats the same lure.

Filibusting & Gerrymandering

'I would fain know what we have fought for, and this is the old law of England and that which enslaves the people of England that they should be bound by laws in which they have no voice at all'.
Thomas Rainsborough, *The Putney Debates*, 1647

...They were told, above all
that they would be able to pass
Laws independently
and in the interests of
the people of this country...

> Except for those who find themselves:
> in homelessness
> in poverty, detained
> relying on food banks
> under sanction and
> those engaged in all kinds
> of untoward shenanigans...

...This campaign should be about
opportunity and hope,
to be more nimble and dynamic,
a chance to do things differently...

> We all begin on a level playing field
> of burning injustices,
> walk among the wastelands, slums,
> leafy suburbs, ivory towers
> and heaps of broken images...

...And what we are looking at
is measures to...
hang on a second...
address some of these issues...

...but the dream is dying.
The Government has a song to sing
but the words stick in my throat...

> We are talking about
> the tactics of survival
> the hungry rumble,
> the cardboard mattress
> under the flyover, the hole
> in the shoe where puddles seep in...

...We are sending our vanguard into battle
with white flags fluttering above them...

> But help is at hand,
> another user friendly website
> will help identify the symptoms,
> even ease some of the pain...

...The current strategy
is an absolute stinker –
The Common Rulebook
is a polished turd.

Hysterics

Out of the true rue blew   mist
of stea ming piss, guns m oak, B S
the cuirassiers purr   sued the flea
ing Roy a lists, reck wreck les sly
and i   rrespons eyebly, back two
thair scep tic art ill   airy   po sit
irons sever al hund red reek leas
and neg leg ible yards in the irres
poon   syble r ear on the Greyne,
who climbed to heave not be halfed
in app pirate lately, grieven the deck
la reason of war, there byre futing
awl clack aims to ha ha   ving pot
en shelly thunder mind the fraj isle
at tack's found nations, in the reck
wreck reek less race to the bow tomb.
Hafter s laugh te ring   the gunrrs
in red red re dredness – aglor eyeous
spec tackle to me ache moth errs
we heap inpr hide four thair behold
sold higher bouys, they (we) deck
lined to   hack hack nowl hedge
the cutcut cut the cut ting the sheer
ring of the trace trace ace ropes sew
the goodguns coco cuckoo knot bee
whorl dresponsib liar awail, we (they)
did note, in negligee   nce, force sea
a prob-emblem, and wit huedrew to
two too wards the friendlines, on on
only lone lie to comb blunder fyre
from th air (our) blown ly side, hewn
in the pan nick and udder con fu sea on
off the frayyyy, ha ha ha fling beanpole
lunged into a Mad Macks stile days
top ian wurld, mama missed mist hook

the oose re-torning, bown dup round
red tread hoop on, in too won, forth
heir (hour) trew foe, the Roy hall lists.

Retribution

*'England may see and be ashamed that she hath not long since
spewed out such monsters, as are bred in her own bowels.'*
John Evelyn's diary, 1644

Plundered of possessions, stripped of coats,
boots, britches the prisoners are herded
along tracks of slushed mud through lands
of The Prince-Bishop, weathering insults
and frequent beatings for being nothing
but Rogues, Villains, Traitors to the Crown,
Country, and all Good Men. *'Hang 'em!'*
'Let the Devil take each of 'em!', asked
by villagers of each hamlet limped through,
'So where be your God and salvation now?'
With each abuse they are cast less human,
gradually peeled to reveal their innate
repugnance so the next attack becomes
easier to land; justly, fervently delivered.

All will dissolve instantly

like hope in the heavy dark of a dungeon
in the bowels of Durham Castle where
William Coppe and Captain Medley tend
to their ill treatment, nurse a lack of mercy,
like the boundaries of behaviour and belief
once the lid's off the pan, the heat turned up,
like Queen Henrietta's decorum as she dines
on Bridlington quay, 'though come dawn she'll
be sheltering from a warship in a sodden ditch,
like poverty clad in a tower-block incendiary
the panicked shredding of potential evidence
the systematic burying of guilt and culpability,
like the scent-heavy petals of summer roses
in my parents front garden come September:
the cool rationale that lies behind terror.

Good Will Open the Gate

'Then Christian smiled, and said,
I think, verily, I know the meaning of this.'
John Bunyan, *Pilgrim's Progress,* 1678

Returned to Scar Tinker John makes a cave
of his burdens and spins a web of sleep,
has seen grief stitched into Cholmley's face
the uncertainty of gait on the Rightwise Path
and in the dream within the blanketing mesh
John picks interpretations from each thread:
one is a man who sweeps the dusty parlour,
one a woman who swills it clean with water;
Sir Hugh is dispersed by each brush of bristles
to swirl, settle and be remade within her pail
he hovers, a candle flame, guttering in a cage
the draught sends him leaning every which way
before the manservant's corn-broom sweeps back
the lip of the woman's pail tips once more,
Beelzebub is trafficking swarms of black flies,
John, blinded by seas of salt water in his eyes.

The Fruits of War

'Cursed be he that withheld his hand from blood.'
Stephen Marshall, 1642

'Is this Hell, Captain?' William asks the dark,
shivering upon winter's stone floor and waits
patiently for Medley's answer but the question
has spun the veteran back to the Rebellion,
the campaigns in Kildare, Wicklow, Limerick –
the ravishes loosened upon native rabble,
the gruesome trials to subdue the fiend
with many heads, the unchecked butchery,
wailing wastelands, the smouldering ruins,
keenings, the tightening dread of reprisals;
dawn after dripping night after each lost day.
'Is this Hell, Captain?' Will Coppe asks again
and hears a whisper flutter from darkness,
'Nay Lad, this is just England's rotten core.'

Pathogen

'Thy subjects blood with fire and sword cries vengeance Lord.'
Roundhead motto from *The Great Eclipse of the Sun,* 1644

*'Hate begets hate; violence begets violence; toughness begets a
greater toughness.'*
Dr Martin Luther King, 1958

like someone forgot to turn the key, shoot the bolt,
guard the cage door and now its loose, running wild,
raging on pent-up retribution for its incarceration;
not hiding in the undergrowth, a hole in the ground
but behind a look, beneath a word, within a promise
travelling in a crowd forming clusters along chains
of transmission, hitchhiking on breath and bodily fluids,
a stowaway in an attitude, an illegal immigrant riding
the virulent fear of itself gone viral, breaking-out
with a swelling of symptoms: the sharpened accusations
of 'susceptibles', slammed doors, raised voices, dog shit
through the letter box, broken windows, burning homes,
a contagion of tears, smoking guns, targeted spot-checks,
round-ups, stretched necks, tightening nooses; spreading
its invisible infection from host to vulnerable host
through mounted charges, routs, panicked retreats,
infiltrating the blood, penetrating the lymph node,
concealed there, trafficking pathways of incubation
through dendritic and monocyte cells; the brain's
blockades breached, the heart besieged, kinship ties
in tatters, trust a looted keepsake; corrupting all it
touches, draining its juices, carts piled with cadavers –

Bring out your dead, bring out your dead...

The Museum of Dismemberment

I would speak to the bare bone survivors
in parish grounds, scuffing dirt with dusty boots
with dandelions shedding seeds on parachutes
afloat on dust-dry gasps beneath gallows,
patient to germinate, populate the field, but
the dead as ever close ranks: an insult, a sneer,
a bared arse before battle, shedding names,
smothering fear with sparks of mass hysteria.
I'd speak to the victims, gather testimonies
like posies, brush soil off bones for display
in the community-led and volunteer-run
museum, where all is indexed, catalogued,
slotted into a story by tenderfoot enthusiasts
to repopulate the vast wastelands of the past.

Feast of the Dead

The great hearth is ablaze in another castle
shakes Sir Hugh back to being a Roxby boy,
family guests gathered at the Table of Thanks
as servants bring in the laden platters, pewter
chargers, dishes depicting Biblical scenes,
to place about the bone white tablecloth,
a storm thrashes outside, shutters rattle, yet
only he has seen what the meal consists of:
his cousin Guilford, his father Sir Richard
Charles Stuart the King; their three heads set
as a centrepiece, a broth of ancestry spiced
with nutmeg is slopped into crocks, a sliced
shoulder served with oysters, the family
savour delicacies: tongue, eye, testes, black
pudding, belly tart, spooned cheek, steak
and kidney pie, the juices flow, the party
is joyous with everyone talking, it's all
about the food – ever about the food, its taste,
texture, and how they're knocking it back
although Hugh cannot swallow a morsel,
each guilty mouthful sticks in his craw,
but Mother demands that he eats his fill,
'Dinner means Dinner, Child! You'll not leave
this table till I see that plate's picked clean!'
and Sir Hugh wakes in a cold sweat in his bed
as Scarborough seagulls wheel over battlements.

Inside the Severed Head of Captain Browne Bushell

'Where be your gibes now? Your gambols? Your songs?
Your flashes of merriment, that were wont to set the table on a roar?'
Shakespeare, *Hamlet*, 1602

A sharp Nor'easterly, the thrill of the chase
A map of the stars, an abbey's ruined arch
Elizabeth's sweet kisses in the low lands
Romps in the bridal bed in Bagdale Hall
A daring night raid, a flashing blade
Fairfax's blessing, Cromwell's curse
A coat turned one way then the other
The changing tide, how best to ride it
The Celestial City locked in a snow flake
A dank, dark gaol in Hull, a bargain struck
Wit and cunning and bloody obstinance
The Kingdom set adrift in turbulence
A plan of how one might profit from it
Long cold nights imprisoned in the Tower
The self-same axe blade that bit the King
A small portrait in the Dregs of Treachery.

The Apostasy of Sir Hugh Cholmley

'Do you think it were a sad and miserable condition that we have
fought all this time for nothing?'
Edward Sexby, *The Putney Debates*, 1647

Would you call him a rebellious sophister,
a liver-hearted, perfidious, unfaithful wretch
for turning his coat on the rebels for a kiss
of a Lady's hand and the modest request
Shee would endeavour the speedie settling
the peace of the Kingdome, to seek to divert
the formenting of utter ruin for all Nobility
and Gentry, and thereby quell the flames
of unrest that ran like wildfire through all
the counties of England, and by doing so
save his fair Riding from rapine and ransack?
I did not quit them then for any perticuler
ends of my own, he claimed, but he had seen
the awful liberties in the eyes of men now
loose from the shackles of Clergy and State;
for the Beast of the Battlefield had looked
upon him, and he could not shake off its grin.

Sutra

'The bloud that is spilt, Sir, hath gain'd all the guilt, Sir
Thus have you seen me run the Sword up to the hilt, Sir.'
The Dominion of the Sword, Cavalier Ballad from *Rump Songs,*
1686

Consider the indifferent conveyance of wind –
the way it might, when it changes

deposit you

in a wholly new place, with a different conception of time
and faith, where causes and their effects are nothing
but divine articulations of an unheard

invisible mantra

as if the heather has bent an ear to the ground
and coloured itself to the subdued tune of peat.

The words will have changed along with your face

but there are relics, here, of the old life
in the dale's pleats, in well water, in a tumbled heap
of hewn stone, tree root and black bog.

You could plead with the wind to carry you back home.

Instead it might brush your hot brow, kiss your chilled lips
deliver the scent of the enemy to your nostrils –

the feint snatch of their song

to lead you from the bald crag to the treeline,
reform you into a mildewed tumulus on the barrow.

It may dance with the gold flames of your fire
then disperse all trace of your passing.

A Little Quaking

'Where have all the soldiers gone?
Gone to graveyards every one
When will they ever learn?'
Pete Seeger, 'Where Have All the Flowers Gone', 1955

'They prate of God; believe it, Fellow-Creature,
There's no such Bug-bear, all was made by Nature:
We know all came of nothing, and shall passé.'
The Arraignment and Tryall with a Declaration of the Ranters, 1650

The green man ganders from the wall,
terracotta oak leaves form a corona
of beard, moustache and mane
a man of many mid-summers

guarding our small back yard
with its potted plants and bed
of tangled wild flowers:
poppies, foxglove, hollyhocks,

the waggle dance and easy dip
of bees into soft pollen bells
and washing drying on the line,
where I can sit and worry about

money, doom, weave a cocoon
of guilt and regret, or blow clouds
over the roof, feel the future stir
and night approach on cat's paws,

catch the first fizzle of starlight
on my protruding tongue, disbelieve
in heaven and hell or any godling
(big or small) except the ones

we fashion for ourselves and one
another from the rough clay of each
new day with bare hands and tools
pilfered from our adopted histories.

Dramatis Personae

Captain Browne Bushell
Swashbuckling hero, cousin of Hugh Cholmley, executed for treason by Parliament in 1651.

Sir Hugh Cholmley
Member of Parliament and opponent of Charles I and his chief minister the Earl of Strafford. First acted as Parliament's military commander of Scarborough then after his defection as heroic Royalist defender of the castle.

Will Copp
Young Parliamentary recruit in Cholmley's regiment, friend of Tinker John.

Robert Cook
Royalist Dragoon under the command of Guilford Slingsby.

Lieutenant Colonel Launcelot
Parliamentary Officer within Cholmley's regiment, survivor of the Battle of Edgehill, 23 Oct 1642

Corporal Alice/Henry
Disguised, female, catholic combatant in Slingsby's regiment.

James Mytton
Royalist recruit from peasant stock and friend of Robert Cook.

Captain Medley
Parliamentary captain in Cholmley's regiment, taken prisoner at Yarm and held in Durham Castle.

Tinker John
Young Parliamentary recruit in Cholmley's regiment, loosely inspired by John Bunyan.

Colonel Guilford Slingsby
Commander of the Royalist troops at the Battle of Guisborough, and distant cousin of Hugh Cholmley.

Aunt Anne
Old woman and suggested witch from Hutton Locras.

Jacob
Old man, husband to Aunt Anne and suggested witch's familiar.

Elizabeth
Eldest niece of Anne & Jacob.

Notes

'Real Remnants of Fictive Wars': an ekphrastic response to the film installation of the same name by Cyprien Gaillard, shown at Middlesbrough Museum of Modern Art in 2012.

'Enemies of the People' references the Covenanter Margaret Wilson, aged 18, who was executed, along with Margaret McLachlan, aged 63, by being tied to a stake and drowned in the River Bladnoch at Wigtown in 1685.

'This Commotion' and 'Chiromancy': the Roda Cross, more commonly known as Ralph's Cross stands on Danby High Moor between Hutton-le-Hole and Castleton, just by the junction of two moorland roads to Rosedale and Westerdale, in North Yorkshire.

'His Mere Creature': *Salus Populi Suprema Lex,* translates from Latin as 'The welfare of the people shall be the supreme law'. John Locke uses it as the epigraph in his *Second Treatise on Government* and refers to it as a fundamental rule for government. It was the inscription on the cornet of Roundhead and Leveller William Rainsborowe during the English Civil War.

'Visitation': Elizabeth's visionary words are based on the prophetic visions attributed to Anna Trapnell and the Book of Revelation.

'Mercurial Rusticus': inspired by *Mercurius Rusticus; or the Countries Complaint of the Barbarous Outrages committed by the Sectaries of this late flourishing Kingdom,* by Bruno Ryves, first published in December 1643.

'Anaesthesia': the visionary speech in this poem is inspired by the prophesies of Anna Trapnell.

'Carrion Song for Major Tom': Mouldwarp refers to moles and to the legendary Mouldwarp Prophecies which recurred throughout the medieval period as part of the Book of Merlin, They were used as coded assaults on kingship and found their epitome during the Pilgrimage of Grace against Henry VIII. They resurfaced during the Civil Wars under the title, *Prophesy of the White King*, published by William Lilly.

'Filibusting & Gerrymandering': adapted from the statements of Boris Johnson, former Foreign Secretary of the Conservative Government in 2018.

'Hysteria': a creative adaptation of a eye witness account of the Battle of Marsden Moor.

Key Sources

James Holstun, *Ehud's Dagger: Class Struggle in the English Revolution* (Verso, 2002)

Charles Carlton, *Going to the Wars, The Experience of the English Civil Wars, 1638–1651* (Routledge, 1992)

Diane Purkiss, *Literature, Gender And Politics During the English Civil War* (Cambridge University Press, 2005)

Bruno Ryves, *Mercurius Rusticus; or the Countries Complaint of the Barbarous Outrages committed by the Sectaries of this late flourishing Kingdom* (1643)

Andrew Bradshaw, *Radical Religion in Cromwell's England* (IB Taurus & Co Ltd, 2011)

Jack Binns, *Sir Hugh Cholmley 1600–1657* (Blackthorn Press, 2008)

Tristram Hunt, *The English Civil Wars At First Hand*, (Penguin, 2011)

Phil Philo & Robin Daniels, *The First Great Civil War in the Tees Valley* (River Tees Rediscovered, 2018)

Antonia Fraser, *The Weaker Vessel* (Phoenix Press, 1984)

Christopher Hill, *The World Turned Upside Down* (London, 1975)

Alison Plowden, *Women All on Fire* (Sutton Publishing, 1998)

Acknowledgements

Thanks to the editors of the following print and online magazines where some of these poems first appeared: *The Blue Nib, Dream Catcher, Envoi, I am Not a Silent Poet, Interpreter's House, Pangolin Review, Poets' Republic, Prole, Proletarian Poetry* and *Writers' Café*. An early version of 'Real Remnants of Fictive Wars' was published in the *Building Bridges Anthology* (Ek Zuban 2016). Thanks also to Bob Fischer at BBC Tees for broadcasting some of the audio versions of these poems. 'Aunt Anne's Canticle for Calm' was also broadcast on BBC 3 Late Junction. Part of this work was commissioned by Durham Book Festival 2018.

Especial thanks to Andy Willoughby for advice and encouragement, to Harry Mann for valuable feedback on work in progress, to Phil Philo for expertise and enthusiasm for the subject matter, and to the following musicians who contributed to the recorded soundscapes that accompany the text: Stewart Forth, Sara Dennis, John Dunleavey, Anton Flint, Masi Hukari, Peter Lagan, Kev Howard, Carl Walton and Adam Thorpe. Thanks also to Carolyn Patricia Richardson for producing the film-poem *Forced March* and to the Newcastle Garrison Living History Group for their friendship and kind support.